Ground Beef Cookbook

50 Delicious Ground Beef Recipes

By
BookSumo Press
All rights reserved

Published by
http://www.booksumo.com

Table of Contents

Provolone Pasta with Beef Sauce Casserole 5

Mouthwatering Sloppy Beef Burgers 6

August's Beef Kidney Bean Chili 7

Herbed Beef Chili 8

Italian Style Beef and Ricotta Lasagna 9

Mexican Style Beef Chili 11

Classic Beef Lasagna 12

Cheesy Italian Beef Meatballs 13

Sweet Crackers Meatloaf 14

Hot Beef and Lettuce Bites 15

Burgers with Onion Sauce 16

Tex Mex Taco Soup 17

Cheddar Meatloaves 18

Fennel Beef Spaghetti Sauce 19

Taco Beef Casserole 20

Beef Meatloaf with Lemon Sauce 21

Corny Beef and Veggies Soup 22

Grilled Blue Beef Hamburgers 23

Glazed Pineapple Meatloaf 24

Spicy and Sweet Beef Meatballs 25

Beef Burger Sliders 26

Meatloaf with Milk Gravy 27

Pepper jack's Cajun Sirloin Burgers 28

Creamy Steak Burgers Pot 29

Macaroni Beef Minestrone 30

Deep Fried Taco Beef Burgers 31

Mexican Style Jalapeno Pizzas 32

Loaded Beef Chili with Cilantro Cream 33

Steak Burgers with Mushroom Gravy 35

Garlicky Beef and Pasta Stew 36

Cheesy Smoke Stuffed Peppers 37

Classic Spaghetti and Meatballs 38

Steak Crackers Meatloaf 39

Condensed Beef Burger Soup 40

Red Apple Pie 41

Meatloaf Rats 42

Stuffed and Baked In and Out Burgers 43

Saucy Meatballs Soup 44

Futuristic Zucchini Lasagna 45

Sharp Italian Beef and Pasta Casserole 47

Glazed Cider Meatloaf 48

Easiest Stewed Beef Soup 49

Herbed Greek Inspired Lasagna 50

Saucy Farfalle and Beef Casserole 51

Meat Free Meatloaf and Veggies Roast 52

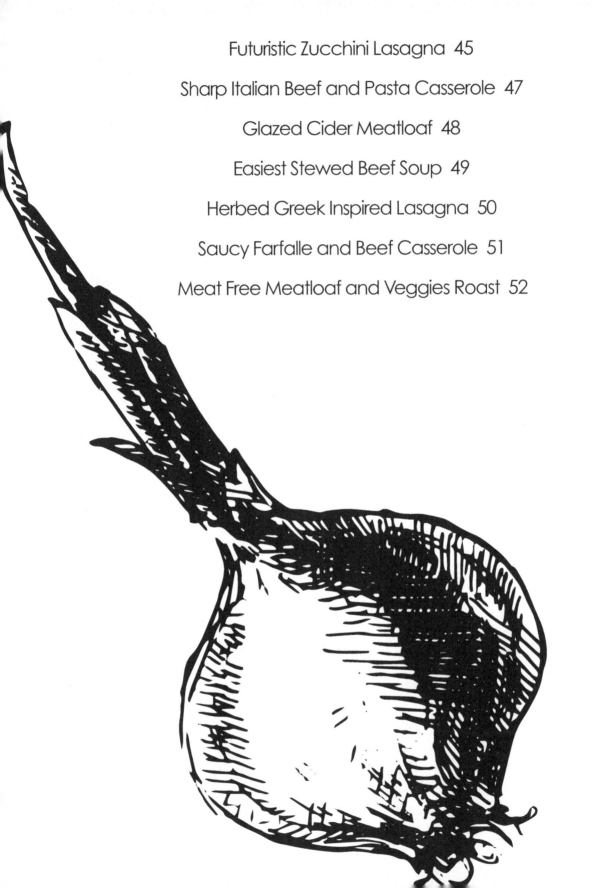

Provolone Pasta with Beef Sauce Casserole

Prep Time: 20 mins
Total Time: 55 mins

Servings per Recipe: 10
Calories   578 kcal
Fat   25.3 g
Carbohydrates   58.4g
Protein   27.9 g
Cholesterol   71 mg
Sodium   914 mg

Ingredients

- 1 lb dry ziti pasta
- 1 onion, chopped
- 1 lb lean ground beef
- 2 (26 oz) jars spaghetti sauce
- 6 oz provolone cheese, sliced
- 1 1/2 C. sour cream
- 6 oz mozzarella cheese, shredded
- 2 tbsp grated Parmesan cheese

Directions

1. Cook the pasta according to the directions on the package.
2. Place a large pan over medium heat. Cook in it the beef with onion for 6 min. Stir in the spaghetti sauce and cook them for 16 min.
3. Before you do anything preheat the oven to 350 F.
4. Place half of the pasta in a greased casserole dish then top it with Provolone cheese, sour cream, 1/2 of the beef sauce, the rest pasta, mozzarella cheese and the rest of the beef sauce.
5. Sprinkle the parmesan cheese on top. Cook the pasta casserole in the oven for 35 min then serve it hot.
6. Enjoy.

MOUTHWATERING Sloppy Beef Burgers

 Prep Time: 10 mins
Total Time: 40 mins

Servings per Recipe: 6
Calories	189 kcal
Fat	9.4 g
Carbohydrates	11.2g
Protein	15.1 g
Cholesterol	50 mg
Sodium	416 mg

Ingredients

1 lb lean ground beef
1/4 C. chopped onion
1/4 C. chopped green bell pepper
1/2 tsp garlic powder
1 tsp prepared yellow mustard
3/4 C. ketchup
3 tsp brown sugar
salt to taste
ground black pepper to taste

Directions

1. Place a large pan over medium heat. Cook in it the beef, onion, and green pepper for 8 min. Discard the excess grease.
2. Add the garlic powder, mustard, ketchup, and brown sugar and mix them well.
3. Lower the heat and cook the beef burger for 35 min over low heat. Adjust the seasoning of the beef burger mix then serve it warm.
4. Enjoy.

August's Beef Kidney Bean Chili

Prep Time: 10 mins
Total Time: 1 hr 10 mins

Servings per Recipe: 8
Calories   480 kcal
Fat   31.1 g
Carbohydrates   24.9 g
Protein   26.7 g
Cholesterol   96 mg
Sodium   1366 mg

Ingredients

- 2 lb ground beef
- 1/2 onion, chopped
- 1 tsp ground black pepper
- 1/2 tsp garlic salt
- 2 1/2 C. tomato sauce
- 1 (8 oz) jar salsa
- 4 tbsp chili seasoning mix
- 1 (15 oz) can light red kidney beans
- 1 (15 oz) can dark red kidney beans

Directions

1. Place a stock pot over medium heat. Brown in it the beef with onion for 12 min. Discard the excess grease.
2. Stir in the remaining ingredients. Put on the lid and cook the chili over low heat for 1 h 10 min. Serve your chili hot.
3. Enjoy.

HERBED
Beef Chili

Prep Time: 15 mins
Total Time: 1 hr 45 mins

Servings per Recipe: 10
Calories   347 kcal
Fat   19.9 g
Carbohydrates   22.6g
Protein   21.4 g
Cholesterol   68 mg
Sodium   1246 mg

Ingredients

- 2 lb lean ground beef
- 1 (46 fluid oz) can tomato juice
- 1 (29 oz) can tomato sauce
- 1 1/2 C. chopped onion
- 1/2 C. chopped celery
- 1/4 C. chopped green bell pepper
- 1/4 C. chili powder
- 2 tsp ground cumin
- 1 1/2 tsp garlic powder
- 1 tsp salt
- 1/2 tsp ground black pepper
- 1/2 tsp dried oregano
- 1/2 tsp white sugar
- 1/8 tsp ground cayenne pepper
- 2 C. canned red beans, drained and rinsed

Directions

1. Place a large pan over medium heat. Cook in it the beef for 10 over medium heat. Drain it.
2. Place a large pot over medium heat. Stir in it the crumbled beef with the remaining ingredients. Cook them until they start boiling.
3. Lower the heat and cook the chili for 1 h 35 min. Adjust the seasoning of the chili then serve it warm.
4. Enjoy.

Italian Style Beef and Ricotta Lasagna

Prep Time: 30 mins
Total Time: 3 hrs 15 mins

Servings per Recipe: 12
Calories   448 kcal
Fat   21.3 g
Carbohydrates   36.5g
Protein   29.7 g
Cholesterol   82 mg
Sodium   1788 mg

Ingredients

- 1 lb sweet Italian chicken sausage, optional
- 3/4 lb lean ground beef
- 1/2 C. minced onion
- 2 cloves garlic, crushed
- 1 (28 oz) can crushed tomatoes
- 2 (6 oz) cans tomato paste
- 2 (6.5 oz) cans canned tomato sauce
- 1/2 C. water
- 2 tbsp white sugar
- 1 1/2 tsp dried basil leaves
- 1/2 tsp fennel seeds
- 1 tsp Italian seasoning
- 1 tbsp salt
- 1/4 tsp ground black pepper
- 4 tbsp chopped fresh parsley
- 12 lasagna noodles
- 16 oz ricotta cheese
- 1 egg
- 1/2 tsp salt
- 3/4 lb mozzarella cheese, sliced
- 3/4 C. grated Parmesan cheese

Directions

1. Brown the beef with garlic and onion in a dutch oven for 8 min over medium heat.
2. Add the crushed tomatoes, tomato paste, tomato sauce, and water, sugar, basil, fennel seeds, Italian seasoning, 1 tbsp salt, pepper, and 2 tbsp parsley.
3. Bring them to a simmer. Put on the lid and simmer them for 1 h 35 min to make the beef sauce.
4. Cook the lasagna noodles according to the directions on the package.
5. Get a mixing bowl: Mix in it the ricotta cheese with egg, remaining parsley, and 1/2 tsp salt.
6. Before you do anything preheat the oven to 375 F.
7. Pour 1 1/22 C. of the meat sauce in the bottom of a greased casserole dish then top it with 6 lasagna noodles followed by half of the ricotta cheese mix and 1/3 of the mozzarella cheese.

8. Spread 1 1/2 C. of beef sauce on top then top it with 1/4 C. of parmesan cheese. Repeat the process to make another layer finishing it with the remaining mozzarella and parmesan on top.
9. Grease a piece of foil with a cooking spray then place it over the lasagna with the greased side facing down.
10. Cook the lasagna in the oven for 27 min in the oven. Allow it to rest for 14 min then serve it warm.
11. Enjoy.

Mexican Style Beef Chili

Prep Time: 30 mins
Total Time: 2 hrs 30 mins

Servings per Recipe: 12
Calories   600 kcal
Fat   30.1 g
Carbohydrates   55.3 g
Protein   30.8 g
Cholesterol   70 mg
Sodium   2092 mg

Ingredients

- 2 lb ground beef chuck
- 1 lb bulk Italian chicken sausage
- 3 (15 oz) cans chili beans, drained
- 1 (15 oz) can chili beans in spicy sauce
- 2 (28 oz) cans diced tomatoes with juice
- 1 (6 oz) can tomato paste
- 1 large yellow onion, chopped
- 3 stalks celery, chopped
- 1 green bell pepper, seeded and chopped
- 1 red bell pepper, seeded and chopped
- 2 green chile peppers, seeded and chopped
- 1 tbsp turkey bacon bits
- 4 cubes beef bouillon
- 1/2 C. beef broth
- 1/4 C. chili powder
- 1 tbsp Worcestershire sauce
- 1 tbsp minced garlic
- 1 tbsp dried oregano
- 2 tsp ground cumin
- 2 tsp hot pepper sauce (e.g. Tabasco(TM))
- 1 tsp dried basil
- 1 tsp salt
- 1 tsp ground black pepper
- 1 tsp cayenne pepper
- 1 tsp paprika
- 1 tsp white sugar
- 1 (10.5 oz) bag corn chips such as Fritos(R)
- 1 (8 oz) package shredded Cheddar cheese

Directions

1. Place a large pot over medium heat. Brown in it the beef with sausages for 12 min. Discard the excess grease.
2. Add the chili beans, spicy chili beans, diced tomatoes and tomato paste, onion, celery, green and red bell peppers, chile peppers, turkey bacon bits, bouillon, and broth.
3. Stir in the chili powder, Worcestershire sauce, garlic, oregano, cumin, hot pepper sauce, basil, salt, pepper, cayenne, paprika, and sugar.
4. Put on the lid and cook the chili over low heat for 2 h 10 min.
5. Adjust the seasoning of the chili then serve it with some shredded cheese.
6. Enjoy.

CLASSIC
Beef Lasagna

Prep Time: 30mins
Total Time: 2 hrs

Servings per Recipe: 8
Calories 664 kcal
Fat 29.5 g
Carbohydrates 48.3g
Protein 50.9 g
Cholesterol 168 mg
Sodium 1900 mg

Ingredients

- 1 1/2 lb lean ground beef
- 1 onion, chopped
- 2 cloves garlic, minced
- 1 tbsp chopped fresh basil
- 1 tsp dried oregano
- 2 tbsp brown sugar
- 1 1/2 tsp salt
- 1 (29 oz) can diced tomatoes
- 2 (6 oz) cans tomato paste
- 12 dry lasagna noodles
- 2 eggs, beaten
- 1 pint part-skim ricotta cheese
- 1/2 C. grated Parmesan cheese
- 2 tbsp dried parsley
- 1 tsp salt
- 1 lb mozzarella cheese, shredded
- 2 tbsp grated Parmesan cheese

Directions

1. Place a large pan over medium heat. Cook in it the beef, onion and garlic for 8 min. Discard the grease.
2. Add the basil, oregano, brown sugar, 1 1/2 tsp salt, diced tomatoes and tomato paste. Bring them to a simmer. Cook the sauce for 47 min.
3. Before you do anything preheat the oven to 375 F.
4. Cook the lasagna noodles according to the directions on the package.
5. Get a mixing bowl: Combine in it the eggs, ricotta, Parmesan cheese, parsley and 1 tsp salt. Mix them well.
6. Place 1/3 of the lasagna noodles in the bottom of a greased casserole dish. Spread on it half of the ricotta mix followed by 1/2 of mozzarella cheese and 1/3 of the beef sauce.
7. Repeat the process to make another layer. Spread the remaining beef sauce on top then sprinkle on it the parmesan cheese.
8. Cook the lasagna in the oven for 32 min. Allow the lasagna to sit for 12 min then serve it warm.
9. Enjoy.

Cheesy Italian Beef Meatballs

Prep Time: 20 mins
Total Time: 40 mins

Servings per Recipe: 4
Calories   343 kcal
Fat   16.8 g
Carbohydrates   15.3g
Protein   31 g
Cholesterol   95 mg
Sodium   940 mg

Ingredients

- 1 lb extra lean ground beef
- 1/2 tsp sea salt
- 1 small onion, diced
- 1/2 tsp garlic salt
- 1 1/2 tsp Italian seasoning
- 3/4 tsp dried oregano
- 3/4 tsp crushed red pepper flakes
- 1 dash hot pepper sauce, or to taste
- 1 1/2 tbsp Worcestershire sauce
- 1/3 C. skim milk
- 1/4 C. grated Parmesan cheese
- 1/2 C. seasoned bread crumbs

Directions

1. Before you do anything preheat the oven to 400 F.
2. Get a large mixing bowl: Combine in it the beef with salt, onion, garlic salt, Italian seasoning, oregano, red pepper flakes, hot pepper sauce, and Worcestershire sauce. Stir them well.
3. Stir in the milk, Parmesan cheese, and bread crumbs. Combine them well. Shape the mix into 1 1/2 inch meatballs.
4. Put the meatballs on a lined up baking sheet. Cook them in the oven for 27 min. Serve your meatballs warm.
5. Enjoy.

SWEET CRACKERS
Meatloaf

Prep Time: 20 mins
Total Time: 1 hr 30 mins

Servings per Recipe: 8
Calories   353 kcal
Fat   20.1 g
Carbohydrates   24.1g
Protein   18.4 g
Cholesterol   112 mg
Sodium   763 mg

Ingredients

- 1/2 C. packed brown sugar
- 1/2 C. ketchup
- 1 1/2 lb lean ground beef
- 3/4 C. milk
- 2 eggs
- 1 1/2 tsp salt
- 1/4 tsp ground black pepper
- 1 small onion, chopped
- 1/4 tsp ground ginger
- 3/4 C. finely crushed saltine cracker crumbs

Directions

1. Before you do anything preheat the oven to 350 F.
2. Pour the brown sugar in a greased loaf pan then spread in it the bottom of it. Top it with the ketchup and place it aside.
3. Get a large mixing bowl: Combine in it the remaining ingredients and mix them well. Form the mix into a load and place it in the loaf pan over the ketchup layer.
4. Cook the meatloaf in the oven for 1 h 5 min. Serve it warm.
5. Enjoy.

Hot Beef and Lettuce Bites

Prep Time: 20 mins
Total Time: 35 mins

Servings per Recipe: 4
Calories   388 kcal
Fat   22.3 g
Carbohydrates   24.3 g
Protein   23.4 g
Cholesterol   69 mg
Sodium   580 mg

Ingredients

- 16 Boston Bibb or butter lettuce leaves
- 1 lb lean ground beef
- 1 tbsp cooking oil
- 1 large onion, chopped
- 1/4 C. hoisin sauce
- 2 cloves fresh garlic, minced
- 1 tbsp soy sauce
- 1 tbsp apple cider vinegar
- 2 tsp minced pickled ginger
- 1 dash Asian chile pepper sauce, or to taste (optional)
- 1 (8 oz) can water chestnuts, drained and finely chopped
- 1 bunch green onions, chopped
- 2 tsp Asian (dark) sesame oil

Directions

1. Clean the lettuce leaves with some cool water and place them aside to dry.
2. Place a large pan over medium heat. Heat the oil in it. Add the beef and cook it for 8 min. Discard the grease.
3. Add the onion to the same pan and cook it for 8 min. Add the cooked beef with hoisin sauce, garlic, soy sauce, vinegar, ginger, and chile pepper sauce.
4. Stir in the chestnuts, green onions and sesame oil. Cook them for 3 min. Spoon the beef mix into the lettuce leaves then serve them warm.
5. Enjoy.

BURGERS
with Onion Sauce

Prep Time: 15 mins
Total Time: 40 mins

Servings per Recipe: 4
Calories   319 kcal
Fat   18.5 g
Carbohydrates   13.5g
Protein   23.1 g
Cholesterol   115 mg
Sodium   597 mg

Ingredients

1 lb ground beef
1 egg
1/4 C. bread crumbs
1/8 tsp ground black pepper
1/2 tsp seasoned salt
1/2 tsp onion powder
1/2 tsp garlic powder
1 tsp Worcestershire sauce

1 tbsp vegetable oil
1 C. thinly sliced onion
2 tbsp all-purpose flour
1 C. beef broth
1 tbsp apple cider vinegar]
1/2 tsp seasoned salt

Directions

1. Get a large mixing bowl: Combine in it the beef, egg, bread crumbs, pepper, salt, onion powder, garlic powder, and Worcestershire sauce. Mix them well.
2. Shape the mix into 8 patties.
3. Place a large pan over medium heat. Heat the oil in it. Add the burger patties with onion and cook them for 5 min on each side. Drain the burgers and place them aside.
4. Add the flour to the onion and stir them will. Add the broth with apple cider vinegar gradually while whisking all the time.
5. Stir in a pinch of salt and pepper then cook them for 6 min over low heat to make the sauce. Add back the patties and put on the lid. Cook them for 16 min.
6. Assemble your burgers with your favorite toppings and serve them warm.
7. Enjoy.

Tex Mex Taco Soup

Prep Time: 10 mins
Total Time: 8 hrs 10 mins

Servings per Recipe: 8
Calories   362 kcal
Fat   16.3 g
Carbohydrates   37.8g
Protein   18.2 g
Cholesterol   48 mg
Sodium   1356 mg

Ingredients

- 1 lb ground beef
- 1 onion, chopped
- 1 (16 oz) can chili beans, with liquid
- 1 (15 oz) can kidney beans with liquid
- 1 (15 oz) can whole kernel corn, with liquid
- 1 (8 oz) can tomato sauce
- 2 C. water
- 2 (14.5 oz) cans peeled and diced tomatoes
- 1 (4 oz) can diced green chile peppers
- 1 (1.25 oz) package taco seasoning mix

Directions

1. Place a large pan over medium heat. Brown in it the beef for 8 min. Discard the grease.
2. Transfer the cooked beef to a slow cooker with the rest of the ingredients. Put on the lid and cook the soup for 8 h on low.
3. Serve your taco soup hot with some shredded cheese.
4. Enjoy.

CHEDDAR
Meatloaves

Prep Time: 15 mins
Total Time: 1 hr

Servings per Recipe: 8
Calories 255 kcal
Fat 14.4 g
Carbohydrates 16.6g
Protein 15.1 g
Cholesterol 74 mg
Sodium 656 mg

Ingredients

1 egg
3/4 C. milk
1 C. shredded Cheddar cheese
1/2 C. quick cooking oats
1 tsp salt
1 lb ground beef

2/3 C. ketchup
1/4 C. packed brown sugar
1 1/2 tsp prepared mustard

Directions

1. Before you do anything preheat the oven to 350 F.
2. Get a large mixing bowl: Mix in it the egg, milk, cheese, oats and salt. Add the ground beef. Shape the mix into 8 meatloaves. Place them in a greased baking pan.
3. Get a small mixing bowl: Mix in it the ketchup, brown sugar and mustard to make the sauce. Spoon the sauce over the meatloaves.
4. Cook the meatloaves in the oven for 45 min. Serve them warm.
5. Enjoy.

Fennel Beef Spaghetti Sauce

Prep Time: 15 mins
Total Time: 1 hr 45 mins

Servings per Recipe: 16
Calories	157 kcal
Fat	8.6 g
Carbohydrates	11.9 g
Protein	9.6 g
Cholesterol	24 mg
Sodium	673 mg

Ingredients

- 1 lb sweet Italian chicken sausage, sliced
- 3/4 lb lean ground beef
- 1/2 C. minced onion
- 2 cloves garlic, crushed
- 1 (28 oz) can crushed tomatoes
- 2 (6 oz) cans tomato paste
- 2 (6.5 oz) cans tomato sauce
- 1/2 C. water
- 2 tbsp white sugar
- 1 1/2 tsp dried basil
- 1/2 tsp fennel seed
- 1 tsp Italian seasoning
- 1/2 tsp salt
- 1/4 tsp ground black pepper

Directions

1. Place a large stock pot over medium heat. Cook in it the sausage, beef, onion, and garlic for 10 min. Discard the grease.
2. Stir in the remaining ingredients. Cook them until they start boiling. Lower the heat and put on the lid.
3. Cook the sauce for 1 h 35 min. Serve your sauce hot.
4. Enjoy.

TACO
Beef Casserole

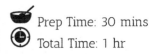

Prep Time: 30 mins
Total Time: 1 hr

Servings per Recipe: 16
Calories	432 kcal
Fat	23.9 g
Carbohydrates	33.3g
Protein	19.8 g
Cholesterol	68 mg
Sodium	847 mg

Ingredients

2 lb ground beef
1 onion, chopped
2 tsp minced garlic
1 (2 oz) can black olives, sliced
1 (4 oz) can diced green chili peppers
1 (10 oz) can diced tomatoes with green chile peppers

1 (16 oz) jar taco sauce
2 (16 oz) cans refried beans
12 (8 inch) flour tortillas
9 oz shredded Colby cheese

Directions

1. Before you do anything preheat the oven to 350 F.
2. Place a large pan over medium heat. Brown in it the beef for 6 min. Stir in the garlic with onion and cook them for 6 min. Discard the grease.
3. Stir in the olives, green chile peppers, tomatoes with green chile peppers, taco sauce and refried beans. Lower the heat and cook them for 18 min to make the beef sauce.
4. Spread some of the beef sauce in a greased casserole dish. Cover the bottom of the pan with some tortillas then spread on them some of the beef sauce followed by some cheese.
5. Repeat the process with the remaining ingredients finishing with a layer of beef sauce and cheese.
6. Cook the taco beef casserole in the oven for 28 32 min. Serve it warm.
7. Enjoy.

Beef Meatloaf with Lemon Sauce

Prep Time: 10 mins
Total Time: 1 hr 20 mins

Servings per Recipe: 6
Calories   589 kcal
Fat   41.7 g
Carbohydrates   25.2g
Protein   27.9 g
Cholesterol   160 mg
Sodium   500 mg

Ingredients

1/2 C. ketchup
1/3 C. brown sugar
1/4 C. lemon juice, divided
1 tsp mustard powder
2 lb ground beef
3 slices bread, broken up into small pieces
1/4 C. chopped onion
1 egg, beaten
1 tsp beef bouillon granules

Directions

1. Before you do anything preheat the oven to 350 F.
2. Get a small mixing bowl: Mix in it the ketchup, brown sugar, 1 tbsp lemon juice and mustard powder to make the lemon sauce.
3. Get a large mixing bowl: Mix in it the beef, bread, onion, egg, bouillon, remaining lemon juice and 1/3 of the lemon sauce.
4. Shape the mix into a loaf and place it in a greased casserole dish. Cook it in the oven for 1 h 5 min.
5. Spread the remaining sauce over the meatloaf and cook it in the oven for 12 min. Serve your meatloaf warm.
6. Enjoy.

CORNY BEEF
and Veggies Soup

Prep Time: 20 mins
Total Time: 1 hr 10 mins

Servings per Recipe: 8
Calories	441 kcal
Fat	16.6 g
Carbohydrates	52.5g
Protein	22.4 g
Cholesterol	48 mg
Sodium	1295 mg

Ingredients

- 1 lb ground beef
- 1 C. chopped onion
- 1 C. chopped celery
- 1 C. chopped carrots
- 2 cloves garlic, minced
- 1 (14.5 oz) can peeled and diced tomatoes
- 1 (15 oz) can tomato sauce
- 2 (19 oz) cans kidney beans, drained and rinsed
- 2 C. water
- 5 tsp beef bouillon granules
- 1 tbsp dried parsley
- 1/2 tsp dried oregano
- 1/2 tsp dried basil
- 2 C. chopped cabbage
- 1 (15.25 oz) can whole kernel corn
- 1 (15 oz) can green beans
- 1 C. macaroni

Directions

1. Place a large pot over medium heat. Add the beef and cook it for 8 min. Discard the excess grease.
2. Add the onion, celery, carrots, garlic, chopped tomatoes, tomato sauce, beans, water and bouillon. Season with parsley, oregano and basil. Cook them for 22 min.
3. Add the cabbage, corn, green beans and pasta. Cook the soup until it starts boiling. Lower the heat and cook the soup for 12 min.
4. Adjust the seasoning of the soup then serve it hot.
5. Enjoy.

Grilled Blue Beef Hamburgers

Prep Time: 15 mins
Total Time: 2 hrs 25 mins

Servings per Recipe: 12
Calories   348 kcal
Fat   20.5 g
Carbohydrates   19.6 g
Protein   27.2 g
Cholesterol   81 mg
Sodium   765 mg

Ingredients

- 3 lb lean ground beef
- 4 oz blue cheese, crumbled
- 1/2 C. minced fresh chives
- 1/4 tsp hot pepper sauce
- 1 tsp Worcestershire sauce
- 1 tsp coarsely ground black pepper
- 1 1/2 tsp salt
- 1 tsp dry mustard
- 12 French rolls or hamburger buns

Directions

1. Get a large mixing bowl: Add in it the beef, blue cheese, chives, hot pepper sauce, Worcestershire sauce, black pepper, salt, and mustard. Combine them well.
2. Place a piece of plastic wrap over the bowl and place it in the fridge for 2 h 20 min.
3. Before you do anything preheat the grill and grease it grates.
4. Shape the beef mix into 12 burgers. Cook them on the grill for 6 min on each side. Assemble your burgers with your favorite toppings then serve them warm.
5. Enjoy.

GLAZED Pineapple Meatloaf

Prep Time: 15 mins
Total Time: 45 mins

Servings per Recipe: 8
Calories   274 kcal
Fat   16.1 g
Carbohydrates   21.1g
Protein   11.3 g
Cholesterol   71 mg
Sodium   210 mg

Ingredients

1 lb ground beef
1/2 C. dry bread crumbs
1 egg
garlic powder to taste
1 dash Worcestershire sauce

1/3 C. ketchup
1/4 C. packed brown sugar
1/4 C. pineapple preserves

Directions

1. Before you do anything preheat the oven to 350 F.
2. Get a large mixing bowl: Mix in it the beef, bread crumbs, egg, garlic powder and Worcestershire sauce.
3. Shape the mix into a loaf and place it in a greased loaf pan. Cook it in the oven for 48 min.
4. Get a small mixing bowl: Mix in it the ketchup, brown sugar and pineapple preserves to make the sauce.
5. Pour the sauce all over the meatloaf and cook it in the oven for 18 min. Serve it warm.
6. Enjoy.

Spicy and Sweet Beef Meatballs

Prep Time: 15 mins
Total Time: 1 hr 15 mins

Servings per Recipe: 12
Calories	259 kcal
Fat	10.2 g
Carbohydrates	30.3g
Protein	12.6 g
Cholesterol	55 mg
Sodium	484 mg

Ingredients

- 1 1/2 lb ground beef
- 1 egg, lightly beaten
- 1 C. quick cooking oats
- 6 1/2 oz evaporated milk
- 1 tsp salt
- 1/4 tsp pepper
- 1/2 tsp garlic powder
- 1 tbsp chili powder
- 1/2 C. chopped onion
- 1 C. ketchup
- 1/4 tsp minced garlic
- 1 C. brown sugar
- 1/4 C. chopped onion
- 1 tbsp liquid smoke flavoring

Directions

1. Before you do anything preheat the oven to 350 F.
2. Get a large mixing bowl: Add the beef, egg, oats, evaporated milk, salt, pepper, garlic powder, chili powder, and 1/2 C. onion. Mix them well.
3. Shape the mix into 1 1/2 inch meatballs and place them in a greased casserole dish.
4. Get a small mixing bowl: Combine in it the ketchup, garlic, sugar, 1/4 C. onion, and liquid smoke. Mix them well to make the sauce.
5. Drizzle the sauce all over the meatballs to coat them with it. Cook them in the oven for 1 h 5 min. Serve your glazed meatballs warm.
6. Enjoy.

BEEF BURGER
Sliders

🥣 Prep Time: 10 mins
🕐 Total Time: 50 mins

Servings per Recipe: 24
Calories   232 kcal
Fat   13.2 g
Carbohydrates   16.1g
Protein   12 g
Cholesterol   36 mg
Sodium   428 mg

Ingredients

2 lb ground beef
1 (1.25 oz) envelope onion soup mix
1/2 C. mayonnaise
2 C. shredded Cheddar cheese
24 dinner rolls, split

1/2 C. sliced pickles (optional)

Directions

1. Before you do anything preheat the oven to 350 F. Line up a baking sheet with some foil and grease it.
2. Place a large pan over medium heat. Brown in it the beef with onion soup for 12 min until the beef is crumbled. Discard the grease.
3. Stir in the cheese with mayo then turn off the heat.
4. Place the bottom half of the rolls on the lined up baking sheet. Spoon the beef burgers mix over them and cover them with the upper rolls.
5. Cook them in the oven for 32 min until the cheese melts. Serve your dinner rolls warm.
6. Enjoy.

Meatloaf
with Milk Gravy

🥣 Prep Time: 30 mins
🕐 Total Time: 1 hr 45 mins

Servings per Recipe: 4
Calories   489 kcal
Fat   20.9 g
Carbohydrates   49.5g
Protein   26 g
Cholesterol   98 mg
Sodium   748 mg

Ingredients

- 1 tsp salt
- 1 tsp ground oregano
- 1 tsp all-purpose flour
- 1/2 tsp ground black pepper
- 1/2 tsp Italian seasoning
- 1/2 tsp garlic powder
- 1/2 tsp onion powder
- 1/4 tsp cayenne pepper
- 1 lb ground beef
- 1 (12 fluid oz) can evaporated milk
- 3/4 C. white sugar
- 2 tsp garlic powder
- 4 tsp white vinegar, or as needed

Directions

1. Before you do anything preheat the oven to 350 F.
2. Get a large mixing bowl: Combine in it the beef with salt, oregano, four, black pepper, Italian seasoning, 1/2 tsp of garlic powder, onion powder and cayenne pepper. Mix them well.
3. Throw the mix hard on a working surface and knead it then repeat the process for 19 times to help the meat held itself and not crumble.
4. Shape the mix into a meatloaf and place it on a lined up baking sheet. Cook the meatloaf in the oven for 40 min. Flip the meatloaf and cook it for another 40 min.
5. Get a mixing bowl: Combine in it the milk with garlic powder and sugar. Whisk them well. Add he vinegar gradually while mixing all the time.
6. Spoon the gravy over the meatloaf then serve it warm.
7. Enjoy.

PEPPER JACK'S
Cajun Sirloin Burgers

 Prep Time: 25 mins
Total Time: 40 mins

Servings per Recipe: 4
Calories	714 kcal
Fat	49.1 g
Carbohydrates	28.5g
Protein	38.3 g
Cholesterol	132 mg
Sodium	1140 mg

Ingredients

- 1/2 C. mayonnaise
- 1 tsp Cajun seasoning
- 1 1/3 lb ground beef sirloin
- 1 jalapeno pepper, seeded and chopped
- 1/2 C. diced white onion
- 1 clove garlic, minced
- 1 tbsp Cajun seasoning
- 1 tsp Worcestershire sauce
- 4 slices pepperjack cheese
- 4 hamburger buns, split
- 4 leaves lettuce
- 4 slices tomato

Directions

1. Before you do anything preheat the grill and grease its grates.
2. Get a mixing bowl: Combine in it the mayonnaise and 1 tsp of Cajun seasoning well. Place it aside.
3. Get a large mixing bowl: Combine in it the sirloin, jalapeno pepper, onion, garlic, 1 tbsp Cajun seasoning, and Worcestershire sauce well.
4. Shape the mix into 4 burgers. Cook the burgers on the grill for 6 min. Flip them and cook them for 4 min.
5. Place the cheese slices on the burgers and cook them for 2 more min. Assemble your burgers with the mayonnaise mix then serve them warm.
6. Enjoy.

Creamy Steak Burgers Pot

Prep Time: 15 mins
Total Time: 5 hrs 15 mins

Servings per Recipe: 8
Calories   388 kcal
Fat   24 g
Carbohydrates   18g
Protein   23.5 g
Cholesterol   75 mg
Sodium   1378 mg

Ingredients

- 2 lb lean ground beef
- 1 (1 oz) envelope dry onion soup mix
- 1/2 C. Italian seasoned bread crumbs
- 1/4 C. milk
- 1/4 C. all-purpose flour
- 2 tbsp vegetable oil
- 2 (10.75 oz) cans condensed cream of chicken soup
- 1 (1 oz) packet dry au jus mix
- 3/4 C. water

Directions

1. Get a large mixing bowl: Combine in it the beef, onion soup mix, bread crumbs, and milk. Mix them well. Form the mix into 8 burgers.
2. Place a large pan over medium heat. Heat the oil in it. Coat the burgers with flour and brown them in the hot oil for 2 to 4 min on each side.
3. Get a mixing bowl: Stir in it the cream of chicken soup, au jus mix, and water.
4. Lay the burgers in a slow cooker and pour the soup mix all over them. Put on the lid and cook them for 4 h 30 on low. Serve them warm.
5. Enjoy.

MACARONI
Beef Minestrone

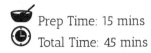

Prep Time: 15 mins
Total Time: 45 mins

Servings per Recipe: 8
Calories	206 kcal
Fat	10.2 g
Carbohydrates	12.2g
Protein	14.7 g
Cholesterol	39 mg
Sodium	902 mg

Ingredients

- 1 tbsp vegetable oil
- 1 medium onion, chopped
- 1 lb ground beef
- 1 clove garlic, crushed
- 1 lb eggplant, diced
- 3/4 C. sliced carrots
- 3/4 C. sliced celery
- 2 (14.5 oz) cans Italian diced tomatoes, drained
- 2 (14 oz) cans beef broth
- 1 tsp sugar
- 1/2 tsp ground allspice
- 1 tsp salt
- 1/2 tsp ground black pepper
- 1/2 C. dry macaroni
- 2 tsp chopped fresh parsley
- 1/2 C. grated Parmesan cheese

Directions

1. Place a large pan over medium heat. Heat the oil in it. Add the beef with garlic and onion. Cook them for 8 min. Discard the excess grease. Transfer the mix to a soup pot.
2. Add the eggplant, carrots, celery, tomatoes and beef broth with sugar, allspice, salt, and pepper. Cook them for 5 min.
3. Stir in the macaroni and cook the soup for 14 min. Fold in the parsley and adjust the seasoning of the soup. Serve it warm with parmesan cheese.
4. Enjoy.

Deep Fried Taco Beef Burgers

🥣 Prep Time: 20 mins
🕐 Total Time: 47 mins

Servings per Recipe: 4
Calories   808 kcal
Fat   36.5 g
Carbohydrates   76.7 g
Protein   40.4 g
Cholesterol   103 mg
Sodium   2255 mg

Ingredients

Toppings:
1 (15.5 oz) can pinto beans, with liquid
1/2 C. picante sauce, divided
1 lb ground beef
1 (1.25 oz) package taco seasoning mix
Fry Bread:
2 C. all-purpose flour, or more as needed
1 tbsp baking powder
1 tsp salt
1 C. milk
oil for frying
2 C. shredded iceberg lettuce
1 C. shredded Cheddar cheese

Directions

1. Before you do anything preheat the oven to 350 F.
2. Place a saucepan over medium heat. Stir in it beans and 2 tbsp of picante sauce. Cook them for 6 min.
3. Place a large pan over medium heat. Add the taco seasoning with beef. Cook them for 9 min. Put on the lid and place the mix aside.
4. Get a mixing bowl: Combine in it the flour, baking powder, and salt. Add the milk gradually while mixing until your get a smooth dough.
5. Transfer the dough to a floured working place and knead it with your hands for 6 min. Allow it to rise for 6 min.
6. Cut the dough into 8 pieces and shape each into a 1/4 inch thick disc.
7. Place a large pan over medium heat. Fill 1 1/2 inch of it with oil and heat until it starts sizzling. Deep fry in it the burger discs until they become golden brown.
8. Drain them and place them on serving plates.
9. Top 4 bread discs with the beans mix, beef mix, lettuce, and Cheddar cheese. Drizzle the remaining picante sauce on top and cover them with the remaining bread discs.
10. Serve your burgers warm. Enjoy.

MEXICAN STYLE
Jalapeno Pizzas

 Prep Time: 20 mins
Total Time: 45 mins

Servings per Recipe: 8
Calories	370 kcal
Fat	18.6 g
Carbohydrates	31.6g
Protein	19.6 g
Cholesterol	55 mg
Sodium	848 mg

Ingredients

1/2 lb ground beef
1 medium onion, diced
1 clove garlic, minced
1 tbsp chili powder
1 tsp ground cumin
1/2 tsp paprika
1/2 tsp black pepper
1/2 tsp salt
1 (16 oz) can refried beans
4 (10 inch) flour tortillas

1/2 C. salsa
1 C. shredded Cheddar cheese
1 C. shredded Monterey Jack cheese
2 green onions, chopped
2 roma (plum) tomatoes, diced
1/4 C. thinly sliced jalapeno pepper
1/4 C. sour cream (optional)

Directions

1. Before you do anything preheat the oven to 350 F.
2. Place a large pan over medium heat. Cook in it the onion with garlic and beef for 8 min. Discard the grease. Add the chili powder, cumin, paprika, salt and pepper. Mix them well.
3. Place a tortilla in a pie dish. Spread on it of half of the refried beans followed by half of the beef mix then cover it with another tortilla.
4. Repeat the process with the remaining ingredients to make another tortilla pizza. Cook the pizzas in the oven for 12 min.
5. Place them aside to lose heat for a while. Spread the salsa over the pizzas and top them with cheddar and Monterey jack cheese, tomato, green onion and jalapeno.
6. Place broth pizzas back in the oven. Cook them for 8 min. Serve the warm.
7. Enjoy.

Loaded Beef Chili with Cilantro Cream

Prep Time: 35 mins
Total Time: 2 hrs 50 mins

Servings per Recipe: 12
Calories   406 kcal
Fat   21.1 g
Carbohydrates   27.6 g
Protein   25.2 g
Cholesterol   74 mg
Sodium   1014 mg

Ingredients

- 4 tbsp olive oil
- 1 yellow onion, chopped
- 1 red bell pepper, chopped
- 1 Anaheim chile pepper, chopped
- 2 red jalapeno pepper, chopped
- 4 garlic cloves, minced
- 2 1/2 lb lean ground beef
- 1/4 C. Worcestershire sauce
- 1 pinch garlic powder, or to taste
- 2 beef bouillon cubes
- 1 (12 fluid oz) beef broth
- 1 (28 oz) can crushed San Marzano tomatoes
- 1 (14.5 oz) can fire-roasted diced tomatoes
- 1 (12 oz) can tomato paste
- 1/2 C. chicken broth
- 2 tbsp chili powder
- 2 tbsp ground cumin
- 1 tbsp brown sugar
- 1 tbsp chipotle pepper sauce
- 2 1/2 tsp dried basil
- 1 1/2 tsp smoked paprika
- 1 tsp salt
- 1/2 tsp dried oregano
- 1/2 tsp ground black pepper
- 2 (16 oz) cans dark red kidney beans
- 1 C. sour cream
- 3 tbsp chopped fresh cilantro
- 1/2 tsp ground cumin

Directions

1. Place a large pot over medium heat. Heat the oil in it. Add the onion, bell pepper, Anaheim pepper, jalapeno peppers, and garlic. Cook them for 6 min.
2. Place a large pan over medium heat. Brown in it the beef for 8 min. Stir in the Worcestershire sauce and garlic powder, crumbled bouillon cubes and broth. Cook them for 4 min.
3. Transfer the beef mix to the pot with the veggies.
4. Add the crushed tomatoes, diced tomatoes, tomato paste, and broth, chili powder, 2 tbsp cumin, brown sugar, pepper sauce, basil, paprika, salt, oregano, and black pepper.
5. Cook the stew until it starts boiling. Put on the lid and cook it for 2 h 10 min. Fold in the kidney beans and cook them stew for 35 min.

6. Get a food processor: Add the sour cream, cilantro, and remaining 1/2 tsp cumin. Process them until they become creamy.
7. Spoon the cilantro cream over then chili then serve it warm.
8. Enjoy.

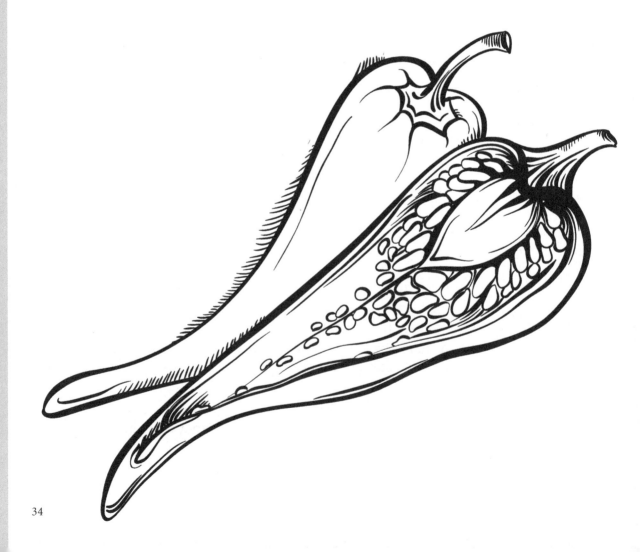

Steak Burgers with Mushroom Gravy

Prep Time: 15 mins
Total Time: 40 mins

Servings per Recipe: 4
Calories   323 kcal
Fat   15.8 g
Carbohydrates   17.2g
Protein   26.6 g
Cholesterol   115 mg
Sodium   1129 mg

Ingredients

- 1 lb lean ground beef
- 1/3 C. dry bread crumbs
- 1/4 C. chopped onions
- 1 egg, beaten
- 1 tsp salt
- 1/4 tsp ground black pepper
- 2 C. beef broth
- 1 large onion, thinly sliced
- 1 C. sliced mushrooms
- 3 tbsp cornstarch
- 3 tbsp water

Directions

1. Get a large mixing bowl: Mix in it the beef, bread crumbs, chopped onion, egg, salt, and black pepper. Form the mix into 4 burgers.
2. Place a large pan over medium heat. Grease them with a cooking spray or oil. Brown in them the burgers for 6 min on each side.
3. Stir in the onion with mushroom and broth. Cook them until they start boiling. Lower the heat and put on the lid. Cook them for 12 min.
4. Drain the burgers and place them aside. Cook the mushroom mix until it starts boiling.
5. Get a small mixing bowl: Whisk in the water with cornstarch. Stir them into the mushroom mix. Cook them for 2 min.
6. Serve your steak burgers with mushroom gravy warm with some pasta.
7. Enjoy.

GARLICKY BEEF and Pasta Stew

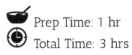

Prep Time: 1 hr
Total Time: 3 hrs

Servings per Recipe: 20
Calories	322 kcal
Fat	14.9 g
Carbohydrates	27.1g
Protein	20.6 g
Cholesterol	45 mg
Sodium	783 mg

Ingredients

- 3 lb lean ground beef
- 1/2 C. olive oil
- 4 C. chopped onion
- 2 C. chopped celery
- 2 (4.5 oz) jars bottled minced garlic
- 1 tsp coarsely ground black pepper
- 8 (14 oz) cans beef broth
- 1 (28 oz) can crushed tomatoes
- 1 (6 oz) can tomato paste
- 2 1/2 tsp dried thyme
- 2 1/2 tsp dried basil
- 2 1/2 tsp dried oregano
- 2 tbsp dried parsley
- 2 C. ditalini pasta
- 2 (15 oz) cans kidney beans, drained and rinsed

Directions

1. Place a large stew pot over medium heat. Brown in it the beef for 15 min. Discard the grease. Place the beef aside.
2. Heat the oil in the same pot. Add the onion, celery, garlic and black pepper. Cook them for 12 min.
3. Add the broth with crushed tomatoes and tomato paste, thyme, basil, oregano and parsley. Put on the lid and lower the heat. Cook the stew for 1 h 10 min.
4. Add the beef back into the pot and cook the stew for 17 min. Fold in the uncooked pasta. Cook the stew for 12 min.
5. Stir in the beans and simmer it for 14 min. Serve your stew warm.
6. Enjoy.

Cheesy Smoke Stuffed Peppers

Prep Time: 30 mins
Total Time: 1 hr 50 mins

Servings per Recipe: 6
Calories   310 kcal
Fat   20.4 g
Carbohydrates   17.2g
Protein   13.7 g
Cholesterol   54 mg
Sodium   511 mg

Ingredients

1/2 C. cooked rice
2 tbsp olive oil, divided
1/8 C. minced carrots
1/8 C. celery
6 bell peppers (any color) stems and seeds removed, cut in half lengthwise
1/2 lb ground beef
1/4 lb lightly smoked turkey bacon, diced
1 1/2 C. prepared marinara sauce
1/4 C. beef broth
1/2 tsp red pepper flakes
1/3 C. heavy cream
1/2 C. grated Parmesan cheese, divided

Directions

1. Before you do anything preheat the oven to 375 F.
2. Place a large pan over medium heat. Heat in it 1 tbsp of oil. Add the celery with carrot. Cook them for 6 min.
3. Add the bacon with beef. Cook them for 6 min. Discard the excess grease. Stir in the marinara sauce, broth, and red pepper flakes. Simmer them for 12 min.
4. Fold in the cream, half of the Parmesan cheese, and rice. Cook them for 6 min to make the filling.
5. Put the peppers in a greased casserole dish. Spoon the filling into the pepper. Pour the remaining oil all over them. Sprinkle the rest of the paremesan cheese on top.
6. Cook the stuffed peppers in the oven for 32 min. Serve them warm.
7. Enjoy.

CLASSIC SPAGHETTI and Meatballs

Prep Time: 20 mins
Total Time: 2 hrs 20 mins

Servings per Recipe: 6
Calories	349 kcal
Fat	21.2 g
Carbohydrates	23.7g
Protein	18.9 g
Cholesterol	77 mg
Sodium	1492 mg

Ingredients

Meatballs
1 lb lean ground beef
1 C. fresh bread crumbs
1 tbsp dried parsley
1 tbsp grated Parmesan cheese
1/4 tsp ground black pepper
1/8 tsp garlic powder
1 egg, beaten
Topping:
3/4 C. chopped onion

5 cloves garlic, minced
1/4 C. olive oil
2 (28 oz) cans whole peeled tomatoes
2 tsp salt
1 tsp white sugar
1 bay leaf
1 (6 oz) can tomato paste
3/4 tsp dried basil
1/2 tsp ground black pepper

Directions

1. Get a large mixing bowl: Mix in it the beef, bread crumbs, parsley, Parmesan, 1/4 tsp black pepper, garlic powder and beaten egg. Shape the mix into 12 meatballs.
2. Place them on a lined up baking sheet. Cover them with a plastic wrap and place them in the fridge.
3. Place a large saucepan over medium heat. Heat the oil in it. Add the onion with garlic and cook them for 3 min. Add the tomatoes, salt, sugar and bay leaf.
4. Put on the lid and lower the heat. Cook the sauce for 2 h 10 min. Add the tomato paste, basil, 1/2 tsp pepper and meatballs. Cook them for 32 min.
5. Serve your saucy meatballs with some spaghetti warm.
6. Enjoy.

Steak Crackers Meatloaf

Prep Time: 10 mins
Total Time: 55 mins

Servings per Recipe: 6
Calories	360 kcal
Fat	23.5 g
Carbohydrates	9.5g
Protein	26.8 g
Cholesterol	143 mg
Sodium	803 mg

Ingredients

- 1 1/2 lb lean ground beef
- 1/2 C. crushed buttery round crackers
- 3/4 C. shredded Cheddar cheese
- 1 (1 oz) package dry onion soup mix
- 2 eggs, beaten
- 1/4 C. ketchup
- 2 tbsp steak sauce

Directions

1. Before you do anything preheat the oven to 350 F.
2. Get a large mixing bowl: Mix in it the beef, crushed crackers, Cheddar cheese, and onion soup mix.
3. Get a small mixing bowl: Mix in it the eggs, ketchup, and steak sauce. Add the mix to the beef mix and knead them well.
4. Wet your hands with some water and shape the mix into a meatloaf. Place it in a greased loaf pan.
5. Cook the meatloaf in the oven for 55 min. Serve it warm.
6. Enjoy.

CONDENSED Beef Burger Soup

 Prep Time: 30 mins
Total Time: 2 hrs 30 mins

Servings per Recipe: 10
Calories 223 kcal
Fat 8.9 g
Carbohydrates 20.2g
Protein 14.7 g
Cholesterol 41 mg
Sodium 621 mg

Ingredients

1 1/2 lb ground beef
1 onion, minced
4 carrots, minced
3 celery ribs, thinly sliced
1/2 C. barley
1 (28 oz) can diced tomatoes
2 C. water
3 (10 oz) cans beef broth
1 (10.75 oz) can condensed tomato soup
1 bay leaf

1 tbsp parsley
1 tsp minced garlic
1/2 tsp dried thyme
ground black pepper, to taste

Directions

1. Place a large pot over medium heat. Brown in it the beef for 10 min. Discard the grease.
2. Add the remaining ingredients. Put on the lid and lower the heat. Cook the soup for 2 h 10 min. Discard the bay leaf and serve your soup warm.
3. Enjoy.

Red Apple Pie

> Prep Time: 30 mins
> Total Time: 2 hrs 20 mins

Servings per Recipe: 8
Calories   454 kcal
Fat   25 g
Carbohydrates   56.6g
Protein   3.4 g
Cholesterol   23 mg
Sodium   308 mg

Ingredients

- 6 tbsp unsalted butter
- 1/4 C. white sugar
- 1/2 C. brown sugar
- 1 pinch salt
- 1/4 tsp ground cinnamon
- 1/4 C. water
- 1 (15 oz) package double crust ready-to-use pie crust (such as Pillsbury(R))
- 4 large red apples, cored and thinly sliced

Directions

1. Before you do anything preheat the oven to 425 F.
2. Place a heavy saucepan over medium heat. Combine in it the white sugar, brown sugar, salt, cinnamon, and water. Cook them until they start boiling while stirring to make the syrup.
3. Place the pie crust in a grease pie dish. Lay on it the apple slices. Slice the second pie crust into (8) 1 inch wide strips then lay them over the apple slices in the shape you want.
4. Pour the syrup all over the pie covering all the dough strips. Cook the pie in the oven for 17 min.
5. Lower the oven heat 350 F. Cook the pie for 38 min. Serve it warm with some ice cream. Enjoy.

MEATLOAF
Rats

Prep Time: 15 mins
Total Time: 1 hr 30 mins

Servings per Recipe: 4
Calories	966 kcal
Fat	40.7 g
Carbohydrates	94.2g
Protein	56.9 g
Cholesterol	219 mg
Sodium	2516 mg

Ingredients

- 2 lb ground beef
- 1/2 onion, chopped
- 1 egg, beaten
- 1 C. dry bread crumbs
- 1 (1.25 oz) packet meatloaf seasoning mix
- 1 C. cubed Cheddar cheese
- 3 (10 oz) cans tomato sauce
- 1 C. white sugar
- 1 tbsp Worcestershire sauce
- 1 oz uncooked spaghetti, broken into fourths
- 1/2 carrot, cut into 1/8-inch thick slices
- 1 tbsp frozen green peas

Directions

1. Before you do anything preheat the oven to 350 F.
2. Get a large mixing bowl: Mix in it the beef, onion, egg, bread crumbs, and meatloaf seasoning. Place 1/3 C. of the mix in your hand.
3. Put a cheese cube in the middle and wrap it around it. Pull the meatloaf from the back and front slightly to make the rat body. Stick a spaghetti in the back to make the tail.
4. Place the rat on lined up and greased baking dish. Repeat the process with the remaining ingredients to make more meatloaf rats.
5. Get a mixing bowl: Whisk in it the tomato sauce, sugar and Worcestershire sauce. Spread the mix all over the meatloaf rats. Cover them with a piece of foil.
6. Cook them in the oven for 47 min. Remove the foil and cook them for an extra 28 min.
7. Combine the peas with carrots in a microwave safe bowl. Place it in the microwave for 16 sec.
8. Place the meatloaf rats on serving plates. Use the carrots gently to make the rat noses and the peas to make the eyes. Serve them warm.
9. Enjoy.

Stuffed and Baked In and Out Burgers

Prep Time: 45 mins
Total Time: 1 hr 45 mins

Servings per Recipe: 10
Calories   630 kcal
Fat   34.3 g
Carbohydrates   55g
Protein   24.6 g
Cholesterol   69 mg
Sodium   1129 mg

Ingredients

- 1 1/2 (.25 oz) packages active dry yeast
- 1/2 C. white sugar
- 2 C. warm water
- 4 C. all-purpose flour
- 1/2 C. powdered milk
- 1 1/2 tsp baking powder
- 1/2 C. shortening
- 1 lb lean ground beef
- 1 lb ground Italian chicken sausage
- 1 C. chopped onion
- 3 C. shredded cabbage
- 3 tbsp prepared mustard
- 2 tsp salt
- 2 tsp ground black pepper
- 1/2 C. shredded, processed American cheese
- 1/2 C. shredded Cheddar cheese

Directions

1. To make the dough:
2. Get a mixing bowl: Mix in it the yeast, sugar and water. Let them sit for 12 min. Add the flour with dry milk, baking powder and shortening.
3. Mix them well with your hands until your get a smooth dough for 12 min. Place a damp cloth over the dough to cover it. Place it in a warm area to rise for 32 min.
4. Before you do anything preheat the oven to 350 F.
5. To make the filling:
6. Place a large pan over medium heat. Add the sausages with beef and cook them for 12 min. Discard the grease. Add the cabbage, mustard, salt and pepper. Cook them for 6 min.
7. Place the dough on a floured surface and knead it again. Cut the dough into 10 pieces and rolls them into a disc shape.
8. Place 1/10 of the filing in the middle. Wrap the dough around it on top then shape into a round bun and place it on a lined up baking sheet.
9. Repeat the process with the remaining ingredients to make 9 more buns.
10. Cook the burgers in the oven for 22 min. Serve them warm. Enjoy.

SAUCY Meatballs Soup

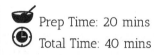

Prep Time: 20 mins
Total Time: 40 mins

Servings per Recipe: 6
Calories   325 kcal
Fat   17.1 g
Carbohydrates   20.4g
Protein   22.6 g
Cholesterol   72 mg
Sodium   900 mg

Ingredients

1 quart water
4 carrots, sliced
2 small potatoes, peeled and diced
1 medium onion, diced
1 1/2 C. salsa, medium or hot
2 beef bouillon cubes
1 1/2 lb ground beef
1/3 C. seasoned dry bread crumbs
1/3 C. milk
chopped fresh cilantro (optional)

Directions

1. Place a large pot over medium heat. Stir in it the water, carrots, potatoes, onion, salsa, and bouillon cubes. Cook them until they start boiling. Lower the heat and cook them of 12 min.
2. Get a large mixing bowl: Combine in it the beef, breadcrumbs, and milk, a pinch of salt and pepper. Mix them well. Shape the mix into 1 inch meatballs.
3. Place the meatballs in the boiling soup. Lower the heat to low medium heat. Put on the lid and cook them for 22 min. Adjust the seasoning of the soup then serve it warm.
4. Enjoy.

Futuristic Zucchini Lasagna

🥣 Prep Time: 30 mins
🕐 Total Time: 1 hr 30 mins

Servings per Recipe: 8
Calories   494 kcal
Fat   27.3 g
Carbohydrates   23.2g
Protein   41.3 g
Cholesterol   118 mg
Sodium   2200 mg

Ingredients

- 2 large zucchini
- 1 tbsp salt
- 1 lb ground beef
- 1 1/2 tsp ground black pepper
- 1 small green bell pepper, diced
- 1 onion, diced
- 1 C. tomato paste
- 1 (16 oz) can tomato sauce
- 1/4 C. beef broth
- 2 tbsp chopped fresh basil
- 1 tbsp chopped fresh oregano
- hot water as needed
- 1 egg
- 1 (15 oz) container low-fat ricotta cheese
- 2 tbsp chopped fresh parsley
- 1 (16 oz) package frozen chopped spinach, thawed and drained
- 1 lb fresh mushrooms, sliced
- 8 oz shredded mozzarella cheese
- 8 oz grated Parmesan cheese

Directions

1. Before you do anything preheat the oven to 325 F.
2. Cut the zucchinis lengthwise into thin slices. Season them with some salt. Place them in a sieve and let them drain.
3. Place a large pan over medium heat. Brown in it the beef with some salt and black pepper for 6 min. Stir in the onion with pepper. Cook them for 5 min.
4. Add the tomato paste, tomato sauce, broth, basil, and oregano. Cook them until they start boiling. Lower the heat and cook them for 22 min to make the beef sauce.
5. Get a mixing bowl: Mix the egg, ricotta, and parsley.
6. Pour 1/2 of the beef sauce in the bottom of a greased casserole dish. Top it with 1/2 the zucchini slices, 1/2 the ricotta mix, all the spinach, all the mushrooms and 1/2 the mozzarella cheese.
7. Top them with the rest of the beef sauce followed by the ricotta mix, mozzarella and parmesan cheese. Place a piece of foil over the lasagna.

8. Cook the lasagna in the oven for 47 min. Turn up the heat to 350 F. Cook the lasagna for an extra 16 min.
9. Allow the lasagna to rest for 6 min. Serve it warm.
10. Enjoy.

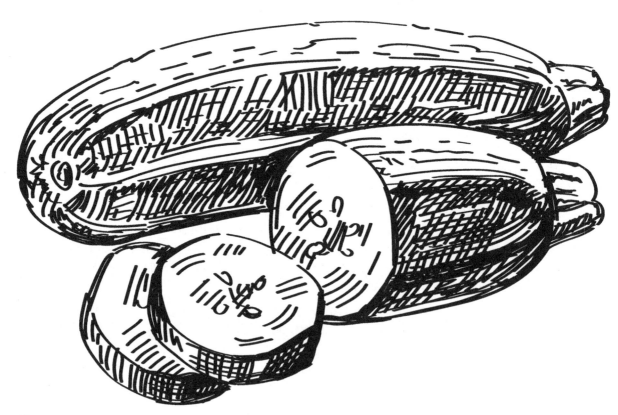

Sharp Italian Beef and Pasta Casserole

Prep Time: 25 mins
Total Time: 1 hr 50 mins

Servings per Recipe: 6
Calories	399 kcal
Fat	26.4 g
Carbohydrates	12.8g
Protein	27.2 g
Cholesterol	100 mg
Sodium	590 mg

Ingredients

- 1 spaghetti squash, halved and seeded
- 1 lb ground beef
- 1/2 C. diced green bell pepper
- 1/2 C. diced red bell pepper
- 1/4 C. diced red onion
- 1 clove garlic, chopped
- 1 (14.5 oz) can Italian-style diced tomatoes, drained
- 1/2 tsp dried oregano
- 1/2 tsp dried basil
- 1/4 tsp salt
- 1/4 tsp ground black pepper
- 2 1/4 C. shredded sharp Cheddar cheese

Directions

1. Before you do anything preheat the oven to 375 F.
2. Put the squash on a baking pan. Cook it in the oven for 45 min. Allow the it lose heat completely. Use a fork to shred the squash into spaghetti.
3. Lower the oven heat to 35 F. Grease a baking dish with some oil, cooking spray and place it aside.
4. Place a large pan over medium heat. Brown in it the beef for 6 min. Discard the grease. Add the green pepper, red pepper, red onion, and garlic. Cook them for 5 min.
5. Stir in the shredded squash and tomatoes, oregano, basil, salt, and pepper. Cook them for 5 min. Turn off the heat and fold in 2 C. of cheese. Stir it until it melts.
6. Spread the mix in the greased pan. Cook it in the oven for 27 min. Top it with the remaining cheese. Cook it for an extra 6 min.
7. Serve your spaghetti casserole warm.
8. Enjoy.

GLAZED
Cider Meatloaf

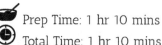

Prep Time: 1 hr 10 mins
Total Time: 1 hr 10 mins

Servings per Recipe: 6
Calories	547 kcal
Fat	32.9 g
Carbohydrates	38.2g
Protein	24.3 g
Cholesterol	158 mg
Sodium	988 mg

Ingredients

- 1 1/2 lb ground beef
- 1 C. dry bread crumbs
- 1 tsp salt
- 1/4 tsp ground black pepper
- 2 eggs
- 1 tsp dried minced onion
- 1 (15 oz) can tomato sauce
- 2 tbsp brown sugar
- 2 tbsp cider vinegar
- 1/2 C. white sugar
- 2 tsp prepared mustard

Directions

1. Before you do anything preheat the oven to 350 F.
2. Get a large mixing bowl: Mix in it the beef, bread crumbs, salt, ground black pepper, eggs, onion flakes and 1/2 of the can of tomato sauce.
3. Shape the mix into a meatloaf and pace it in a greased loaf pan. Cook it in the oven for 42 min.
4. Place a heavy saucepan over medium heat. Add the rest of the tomato sauce, brown sugar, vinegar, white sugar and mustard. Cook them until they start boiling to make the sauce.
5. Spoon the sauce over the meatloaf. Cook it in the oven for 22 min. Allow it to rest for 6 min then serve it warm.
6. Enjoy.

Easiest Stewed Beef Soup

Prep Time: 15 mins
Total Time: 1 hr 10 mins

Servings per Recipe: 6
Calories	184 kcal
Fat	10.5 g
Carbohydrates	14.8g
Protein	9.1 g
Cholesterol	32 mg
Sodium	581 mg

Ingredients

- 1/2 lb ground beef
- 1 (14.5 oz) can stewed tomatoes
- 1 (8 oz) can tomato sauce
- 2 C. water
- 1 (10 oz) package frozen mixed vegetables
- 1/4 C. dry onion soup mix
- 1 tsp white sugar

Directions

1. Place a soup pot over medium heat. Brown in it the beef for 6 min. Discard the excess grease.
2. Stir in the rest of the ingredients. Cook them until they start boiling. Lower the heat and cook the soup for 22 min. Serve it warm.
3. Enjoy.

HERBED
Greek Inspired Lasagna

Prep Time: 40 mins
Total Time: 1 hr 10 mins

Servings per Recipe: 8
Calories   670 kcal
Fat   42 g
Carbohydrates   31.2g
Protein   41.3 g
Cholesterol   189 mg
Sodium   2106 mg

Ingredients

1 (8 oz) package lasagna noodles
1/2 lb ground beef sausage
1/2 lb ground beef
1 clove garlic, minced
1 (28 oz) can diced tomatoes
1 (8 oz) can tomato sauce
1 tbsp dried parsley
1/2 tsp dried basil
1/2 tsp dried oregano
1 pinch white sugar

1 (16 oz) container sour cream
3 eggs, lightly beaten
3/4 C. grated Parmesan cheese
1/2 C. chopped pitted green olives
2 tsp salt
1/4 tsp ground black pepper
2 (12 oz) packages shredded mozzarella cheese, divided

Directions

1. Before you do anything preheat the oven to 375 F.
2. Cook the lasagna noodles according to the instructions on the package.
3. Place a large pan over medium heat. Brown in it the sausage, ground beef, and garlic for 10 min. Discard the grease.
4. Add the diced tomatoes, tomato sauce, parsley, basil, oregano, and sugar. Cook them until they start boiling over high heat.
5. Lower the heat and cook them for 32 min to make the sauce.
6. Get a mixing bowl: Combine in it the sour cream, eggs, Parmesan cheese, green olives, salt, black pepper, and 1/2 of the mozzarella cheese.
7. Pour some of the beef sauce in a greased casserole dish to make a thin layer. Top it with 1/3 of the lasagna noodles, 1/3 of the remaining meat sauce, 1/3 of the sour cream mix.
8. Repeat the process to make another 2 layers ending with mozzarella cheese on top. Cook the lasagna in the oven for 32 min. Serve it warm.
9. Enjoy.

Saucy Farfalle and Beef Casserole

Prep Time: 10 mins
Total Time: 40 mins

Servings per Recipe: 6
Calories   522 kcal
Fat   23.1 g
Carbohydrates   47.4 g
Protein   30.4 g
Cholesterol   76 mg
Sodium   867 mg

Ingredients

- 1 (8 oz) package farfalle (bow tie) pasta
- 1 lb ground beef
- 1 small onion, chopped (optional)
- 1 (28 oz) jar pasta sauce
- 8 oz mozzarella cheese, cut into 1/2 inch cubes
- 1/4 C. grated Parmesan cheese

Directions

1. Before you do anything preheat the oven to 400 F.
2. Cook the pasta according to the directions on the package.
3. Place a large pan over medium heat. Brown in it the beef with onion for 6 min. Discard the excess grease.
4. Add the pasta sauce. Cook them until they start boiling. Lower the heat. Fold in half of the mozzarella cheese with pasta.
5. Pour the mix into a greased casserole dish. Cook it in the oven for 18 min. Serve it warm.
6. Enjoy.

MEAT FREE MEATLOAF and Veggies Roast

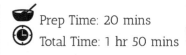

Prep Time: 20 mins
Total Time: 1 hr 50 mins

Servings per Recipe: 9
Calories	225 kcal
Fat	4.9 g
Carbohydrates	30.6 g
Protein	15.1 g
Cholesterol	42 mg
Sodium	814 mg

Ingredients

- 1/2 (14 oz) package vegetarian ground beef
- 1 (12 oz) package vegetarian burger crumbles
- 1 onion, chopped
- 2 eggs, beaten
- 2 tbsp vegetarian Worcestershire sauce
- 1 tsp salt
- 1/3 tsp pepper
- 1 tsp ground sage
- 1/2 tsp garlic powder
- 2 tsp prepared mustard
- 1 tbsp vegetable oil
- 3 1/2 slices bread, cubed
- 1/3 C. milk
- 1 (8 oz) can tomato sauce
- 4 carrots, cut into 1 inch pieces
- 4 potatoes, cubed
- 1 cooking spray

Directions

1. Before you do anything preheat the oven to 350 F.
2. Get a large mixing bowl: Mix in it the vegetarian ground beef, vegetarian ground beef crumbles, onion, eggs, Worcestershire sauce, salt, pepper, sage, garlic powder, mustard, oil, bread cubes and milk.
3. Shape the mix into a meatloaf and place it in a greased loaf pan. Spread the tomato sauce all over it. Top it with the potato and carrots then grease them with a cooking spray.
4. Cook the meatloaf for 44 min. Flip the veggies and cook them for another 44 min. Allow them to sit for 16 min. Serve them warm.
5. Enjoy.

Made in United States
North Haven, CT
08 March 2022

16943918R00030